TARGETED F

preface

Diane talks candidly and frankly about her experience as a so-called targeted person, which is actually a divergent or an ascended being.

She explains how her psychic abilities and new age interests pushed her into a position of danger. How she overcame the life-threatening situations and the impact it made on her life.

Targeted from birth, SRA victim, known in the UK as "Psychic Dee Clare", in Jamaica as "Tiffany" and the Ukraine "Ді Клер" placed her in the spotlight and the centre of mystic, magic manipulation and altered reality. Her experiences include face offs with the Italian mafia,

Jamaican mafia and UK special branches. Throughout the most difficult times Diane held on to her beliefs in Christ Consciousness and through her faith maintained her emotional stability.

Diane shares her insight into aspects of black magic rituals that will amaze you, satanic ritual abuse and how it is used to influence society. How our leaders, politicians and those in positions of power are motivated and controlled by inter dimensional beings. Her knowledge and experience are likely to open your eyes to an entirely new world.

As we approach a shift in energy, change in consciousness, the planet is in need of high vibrational empaths for us to arrive collectively at a common goal of world peace and love.

SUCH A SENSITIVE SOUL

From the early age of 3, I recall being aware of spirit. Not only during my dreams but in the reality of daily life. Life was very complicated, a typical Jamaican home filled with drama. As a young child I sensed the energy of people. Adults appeared with a cloud over them that I quickly used to decide whether or not to trust them. The cloud I recognised as an aura within the depth of my mind... colour beautiful colour. It was the only sense of peace that I could find from day to day. I loved to daydream, nothing changed there, I would imagine little energies or lights around me as I closed my eyes. A red hue would fill my space, switching from red, yellow to orange, in the background, I could hear shouting and arguing, the space in my mind was peaceful. This trait saved me from the TI external noise.

I remember vividly walking down the street with my mother pulling a trolley behind me singing "we are all at the co-op now" from the co-op advert on the tv. Little did I know that the co-op would many years later pull trolleys around me. or TR loll, lick, pop... Little did I know that they were already at this early stage vibrating me on the 55 frequencies.

I always felt alien to my siblings, this went on for years. Christmas and birthdays I went along but somehow, I always felt like the odd one out. The outcast and people would ask my mother. "Is she yours?" they noticed I was aloof from my brothers and sisters. I wanted to join in and be part of the family, sure enough, we played together yet on a spiritual plane we were miles apart.

I struggled to eat a full meal and leftovers I would assign for the spirits or the Gods. I still have bizarre eating habits. I was never particularly fond of food. I recall seeing the Egyptian and Aztec symbols for the first time during a history lesson and fell in love with the symbols. I felt an immediate connection, I recall spending a long-time painting and drawing loving artwork for fun.

I observed others keenly, a people watcher some would say, observing nuances, little things about the way they walked, dressed and talked. It felt surreal, I was shy so it felt easier to watch than join the activities. I felt comfortable sitting outside of the groups and circles, equally loved the excitement of a joint project or outing.

JESUS ALWAYS LOVED ME

At the age of 7, I attended a healing conference with my aunt Gloria Jesus healers came to town in a makeshift circus tent. My cousin suffered with severe disabilities so we took him to the healing revival. It felt so weird, I recall it was full of hundreds of people hoping to heal their loved ones. It didn't heal him, but I imagine now looking back it may have given him some comfort. If I truly believe in the power of the spirit as I do then I know it changed an aspect of his life for the better. I felt the energy of the crowds, the sheer excitement as the healers touched the individuals. Never before had I felt anything like this, it was amazing.

Oh, they watch us, all of us. Everything we do and say, however, I can assure you that this starts way before you realise and it follows from one generation to the next. We own traits and gifts that the entities are aware of. I say entities, this is bigger than the elites, even they are targeted. Do you really believe that some of the elites really want to be in the situation they are in? We are all born into different families and lifestyles for various reasons. Once you wake up to the illusion of this world you are faced with all of your fears. A process designed to put you back into sleep mode, whereby you can be controlled. The beast is faced with the role of keeping humanity entertained to enable "IT" to jump from one body to another. We are merely vessels or mediums for another race, alien race to use and recycle. By recycling, we live to die and then reincarnate and repeat the process over again. The point that you wake up, the ascension point, you become a "so-called" target. Actually, if you look back at your life you soon realise that nothing has changed. You have changed, you see through all the subtle synchronicities, the colours that people wear, the strange objects that they carry and all the various ways that those with the "knowledge" try to use to take advantage of the 'sheeple'.

How did I cope? Well, in the early days I found myself thinking a lot, trying to weigh up what was really going on. In 2017 around April, it felt as if I had been dropped into a computer game. My reality altered immensely. The movies at the cinema seemed directed at me e.g., Paddington's big adventure and Jumanji.

The songs on the radio felt as if they were directed at me, regardless of the station, and the DJ's seemed to be talking directly to me. I watched my bedroom and bathroom layout on Eastenders and snippets of my life on Casualty. Little did I realise that my soul was wired to the DJ's and the music industry. It was completely surreal and at that point, I realised that we are the source for the tv programmes that we are addicted to. I had always known that the tv was designed to watch or study our behaviour, then modify it. The media, well, of course, it is designed to keep the illusion going.

NON-HUMAN ENTITIES WATCH US

I should introduce at this stage the black magicians. The entities will use humans who have offered their services to the dark forces. Obeahman, Wicca man, occultist, and Satanists, they are the guardians of the realm. Their beliefs and practices keep the matrix intact. Their top clients are individuals who are involved in drugs, gun crimes and celebrity status. The system matches culture to culture, "they" (the controllers) use the same culture to play the cat and mouse game. The hierarchy ranges from military to mafia to magicians. They work for the dark forces and use astral projection and telepathy to tap into lightworkers and unsuspecting individuals. They are minions for the dark energies to control the Christs or X-men, higher vibration individuals used to ensure that humanity is completely asleep. The groups of people who have advanced psi or the potential to have authentic psi are identified by tests during education. The education system will reprogram the child to forget their gifts and fall asleep or ZZZ. The group of people who want to live piously good lives against the grain of the majority are cajoled into participation by "agent provocateurs' '. The turn up at school or during college, today the influencers are internet famous or tv famous. The minions are not particularly important to the plan, they are used to keep "divergent" in check. The reward is often through money, plea bargain, food vouchers whatever they can get away with paying. I watched in total shock as the Waitrose vans pulled up to play with my gang stalking neighbours with supplies, knowing full well they could barely afford Aldi.

Returning from London I overheard the team waiting to meet me off the coach to mention that I had cost them more money than anyone ever on this programme. I was just being me, standing my ground caused a real issue, which led me to believe that a lot of the truthers or conspiracy theorists are paid opposition. It felt as if I was a terrorist or a threat to society. I giggled, they obviously felt intimidated. Only then did I realise that I possessed abilities way beyond even my comprehension.

I was a natural intuitive, the gifts were innate and I had no real control, initially over how I used them or in-depth understanding of the type of damage they could cause. Other people were aware of me as they flocked me with such velocity it could only be spiritual. The targeting programme surprised me to be completely honest because I had no idea that I could function on such a level. I had two things to prove from this point on, 1. we are born equal, 2. God the Creator existed and is alive and well. As this planet is a free-will planet it turns into a game of power or game of thrones. The phrases that are used include GOT for different celebrity names that are used to convey situations from one party to another, across countries and teams. No surprise that Emilia Clarke shares the same birthday and surname as me, mother called Jennifer Clarke.

Energy, fields of energy shifting around in the ether, formless until you give it thought. You give it strength and breathe life into it. Words and numbers can create form once absorbed into our consciousness. Eg. injustice has many different meanings. In as in the body, Jamaica US and US entities using your body, ICE on ice. Words can look innocent but form a threat to the person on the receiving end depending on your perception. The universe according to Tesla vibrates using numbers, the targeting vibrates with the numbers 13, 31, 23, 11 and 17. The colours are pink, purple, green, light blue and navy blue. The black magicians work santeria and black magic, they are confident of their work and that they will manipulate your life and decisions. They use a variety of methods to include blood sacrifice rituals, sex rituals and violence. Unfortunately, violence seems to pay out the greater sum in the 3D physical world. The entities are transferred from one person to another during sexual intercourse. Anal sex is a powerful transference of spiritual energies through the combination of feces, blood, and semen. As this toxic substance creates bacteria, methane gas, it is from the chemical combination of the bacteria the demon manifest. Hence the correlation between waste, garbage, and magic.

The entire system is built around the targeted individual game. T-shirts, t-cup are examples of how the T is woven into the fabric of society. They call it hidden in plain sight for obvious reasons. The perp or stalker involved is merely a vessel being used in the same way that the individuals are tormented. Some of the humans do not realise that they are being used, they have made vows with the dark side and to break the vows would mean death in very violent ways.

The child sacrifice, pedophilia is the foundation of the entire matrix. The children are damaged at the young age leading to the formation of alters. The alters do not know each other, I recall one of my most famous perp talking each time with a different voice, eyes changing colour, although I would link this to the use of drugs. Fear alone keeps the perp locked into the agreements; they have been tricked into selling their soul to Satan. Even talking about it causes a great deal of fear, shame, and confusion. The humans are being manipulated on both the light and the dark side. The promise is wealth for the dark and freedom for the light, both endure a similar amount of persecution. The wealth that is promised is not always paid out, it all depends on the decision of the Club, which is subject to change at any time.

The way to battle or fight back is to hand the situation to the Creator and keep positive and healthy. The more creative and outgoing the better, travelling also changes the frequency, it cuts the ties and the spells as the spirit tries to find or relocate the individual. Remember also that the dark forces are in a lower frequency vibration, often drug addiction, mental health issues, depression. The more upbeat and positive, the more difficult it is for them to keep the attachment with you. You will be enticed to join groups or enter into situations. Remember there are many different factions at play, each player with its own agenda.

The Santeria black magic will stir up negativity in your atmosphere, Facebook is used to access the soul of the persons you are friends with. YouTube to "recommend for you" the programming of your subconscious. The occultist can transfer entities to troll or attack you. Your family members turn against you or pretend to be with you, people at work harass you and envy you. Ignore, take no notice and focus on your goals, this is the best revenge. The GAME is designed to crush your spirit, snatch your self-esteem and transfer it to clones. Then you play the game with the perps. There are entities here to assist humanity, some of the people who appear in your life are there to help you. The number frequency has been in existence forever and a day. 22, 23, 33. It becomes easier to feel the presence of the entity. Also, it knows your spirit, as you walk through the streets or go about your business it will avoid you.

THE FIFTH DIMENSION

Welcome to the 5th dimension. These entities have been in existence since creation, it is the technological revolution that has provided the portal for travel between different dimensions. Stop for a minute and take a look at the people walking along the high street. Prescription drugs, alcohol, party drugs, junk food, sweets and chocolates, all provide portals and gateways between dimensions. Rolls, sausage rolls, toilet rolls the roll is a portal for entities to shift from one vibration to another.

Whilst you are being profiled prior to being aware of the covert operation to monitor you, individuals ask you questions about your preferences. If you look back you can see the process repeating itself since your earliest recollections. If you discuss with a person that you read the information on the internet, say Yahoo, then this is the method that your handler will use to contact you.

If you stop reading the headlines the transfer of information occurs on the road using trucks, car stickers. One thing that no target has mentioned to date is that not all of the messages are negative, in fact, a great deal of the messages is positive and guiding you towards your happiness. The glass is half full or half empty, it is actually based on your own beliefs and perceptions. When bombarded with energy the brain freezes and throughout the frozen period it is difficult to locate your reality. The key thing to remember is that you create your life and have ultimate responsibility, it is your choice. The freeway as they call it means that you have set yourself free and society then tries to close in on you to deter you or distract you from making positive changes.

The individuals set up to harass you are also being harassed, and should they fail to drive you crazy, all the energy and negativity returns to destroy their lives. The media in the middle are responsible for causing what is known as fog. To prevent you from ascertaining the best direction for you.

This is where the prayer and positive affirmations step in the more positive and clear the less impact the newly acquired attention can have on you. They say dead because at this point you have passed the point of return. According to bible literature, the Creator allows Lucifer so much time to harass and chase you, once this time has passed, he no longer has the right to. This doesn't stop Lucifer from trying to deceive you, and convince you that you are in it forever. Remember time is up, not for you but for the evil one, the serpent is cut away from you as you ascend to a higher frequency. The beast will not divulge this information for you, it is for you to work it out.

FINANCIAL MARKETS

Their finances are linked to yours; they use terms to tell you. It is currently called the fx, foreign exchange or ft financial times facetime. The reason being the very entities that they conjure up require an outlet or access to your soul to complete the mission. They become your owner and have rights to your spiritual wealth. In the event that the victim, we use the word loosely, is not responding in a low vibration manner, the entity struggles and will go back to the sender. This is when you hear of overdose and other complicated deaths or terrible ritual killings. The more that you express yourself the less power the dark forces have over you, as it is their mission to silence you. Hence the silence of the lambs. The Dad figure assigned to you will provide you with clues this is a person who is living and breathing on this planet. It is better to pretend that you do not see some of the clues but note them. As your every thought and action is being fed into computation to plot your most likely course of action.

This computation can give a detailed picture of your habits and the likely decision route that you will take when faced with various situations. The system will know or at least predict to some extent which direction to take. The beauty of silence is that the computations become distorted and over a period of time it becomes increasingly difficult to map your mind plans. It is a very interesting programme and quite fascinating how intricate it is, also how people are so easily manipulated and controlled. The level of torture drives individuals to commit suicide or join the gang of crazy individuals.

The majority of conversations "street theatre" carries on around you to intimidate you and force you to stay home for fear of going out and about, at this stage, it is clear to you that the targeting is, in fact, real and you picking up on who is involved. It is used to see whether you can be controlled or changed into a bird or butterfly, sacrifice or suicide. A great deal of the perps are drug dealers, sick people, the drunks, drug addicts. Families are oppressed generation after generation. The spirit entity can pick them up and spot an individual a mile away regardless of your location. You would be very surprised to find that the demons have the ability to jump from person to person, bird or animal.

The beauty of writing and creativity, it cuts all the shackles that are holding you into these situations, this is why the targeting is full on, purely to cause confusion and change the way you feel about yourself and think about the world. The phone and computers are used to draw you back into the lower frequency. The 'Keep Calm' slogan is one of the key ways or clues the puppet masters have given society for protection. However, due to the increase in prescription medication, alcohol and drug use it has become difficult for individuals to control their emotions. The key to the entire system is your emotional vibration and whether you can control your feelings.

This is where I draw reference to child trafficking and abuse. The feelings of demonic power become addictive, yet at the same time if the demonic entities are not constantly fed the individual becomes the object of abuse. The obeah and voodoo rituals call for excrement, blood, and torture, the demonic entities will require constant attention to continue providing the material possessions the individual requested. After a period when the material possessions no longer satisfy the desires of the hosts and the individual is ready to leave, the entities resist. I have witnessed individuals under the devil's powers cry and break down when they fail to acquire the attention of their victim or sacrifice for the big boss. The sexual immorality can also cause sexually transmitted diseases, this is breeding ground for demonic entities, if you can imagine bacteria cellular growth, in the same manner, the number of entities multiply.

As we walk through this life, we never truly know our history, however, we know when we are here to make changes to the vibration of the universe. We look beyond the day to day and contemplate what we can do with the system to create a positive impact on the future for the next generation. We consider other children as being our own and make a decision to do the right thing. Regardless of the consequences, in my situation. I completely lost all material positions to illustrate my point.

We can't all be bad; it only requires one person to make the change. Peaceful in our approach, thoughtful in our actions, slow to take offence, humorous and laugh at some of the situations. Right now, we are evolving and changing, it is a good time to be here, we are going to be on the history tablets or chips. Chips...Fish and chips, is a term used to describe us. Lol. We are fish in the ocean and chipped. They are desperately trying to chip our child; I hand her to father God to put her in his heavenly light. To dismantle all chips and technology in the mighty name of Yahushua. I ask also that you release Father to all individuals who are chipped and want to change the feelings they are going through. Thank you, Father. I know that your word is true and would not return to me void. As I type this, I can feel the chip in my back shifting and aching, it is really upset and doesn't want to leave. No choice, it must go as I have free will and my will is with the highest power, the light. The implants I feel are actually in the foodstuffs that we eat.

This is the typical manner in which I would talk and pray over my children when we were being challenged by outside forces.

NO CONSENT TO LOW VIBRATIONAL AGREEMENTS

I cancel all soul contracts made by others against my children with or without consent through covert consent agreements. She is a child of God and free to live her life making her own choices and decisions. Everything that placed money on the table to her detriment, Father I ask that you store the finances in spirit and hand it to my children in this lifetime. This is a mother's call for her children. In the way that I love others, Father I ask that you do the same for my children and provide love for them. The way in I forgive the evildoers Father I ask that you forgive me and my children of all sin. This Father you can do, we only need to ask in the name of Yahushua.

Father the slumber was long and it was a painful feeling waking up, I thank you for allowing me the opportunity to work with you. Through this experience, I trust that I have been a good example for those who doubted the Creator, those who lost faith through unbelief.

The day that I left for Milan the Leicester Mercury ran a big headline, Outfoxed. They seriously felt they had set up my departure out of the country, the spell work had no impact on me whatsoever. I realised that I could change the world with my vision and pure heart. The feeds in Yahoo mentioned guns and shootings. All the people who spoke to me mentioned guns, shooting in the back of the head. Three different conversations over a period of three days. This is how desperate these beings were to fill me with terror. Beings, inter-dimensional beings controlling humanity.

Information shared in real-time on the WhatsApp and dark web, it forms part of the occult and the pictures are shared instantly. Teams are set up to create events around you that appear to be opportunities; however, each member of the team is assigned to you to confuse and distract you, or waste your time. Your reality is altered as if on an 'LSD' trip. Everything appears surreal, the colour of the sky and vans pulling up.

You notice nuances in logos, t-shirts and clothes with 24/7, EA and the North Face, to remind you that you are constantly monitored or targeted. People sit next to you and hold random images; for example, on the plane the young female next to me drinking orange juice, The various people in the hotel drinking orange juice. OJ spent many years selling drugs. It was this spirit that they spell casters intended to transfer to me, as in the Bible whereby the family members load the sacrificial goat sins and send it off to wander in a field. This was the same effect that the siblings attempted to send to me to confuse my life.

INTERNATIONAL AGENDA

On arrival in Jamaica Team 1 sat in the main bar area, they were pleasant and spoke passionately about the medical marijuana show in an attempt to attract me to the exhibition and again fill my aura with narcotics. Every effort was made to destroy my reputation and livelihood.

I could understand strangers, but I found it hard to come to terms with the fact that it was my very own family members. Funnily enough, the Canadians were named Thomas, Markum and they happily went through using all the subliminal names, NLP and numerology. The names are used to open the portals for the individuals who are involved in the game. All that is required to be your opponent is to have negative emotions towards you. They are not conscious of what you are experiencing, each person is going through their own difficulties.

The main guy assigned to be my hook or handler offered me a Pattie and a drink, he desperately wanted me to eat meat or pastry to break my fast. Even the plane offered me apple pie and a Twix, their way of showing allegiance to the game. Everyone appears to be involved, to create a feeling of paranoia. I arrived in

Montego Bay, decided to call Nick to see if he was available to speak. He hung up the phone. Nick is the landlord of the property that I rented in Jamaica, whilst living in social housing in the UK. This was the reason the perps insinuated for my treatment. Nick was actually a major play in the co-op behind my oppression.

The targeting itself I could deal with, what I learned was that the people involved in the game had at some point been targeted. They decided that it was too lonely or too difficult and traded their family member for a slice of the action, little did they know that they would be expected to make a sacrifice going forward.

As you can see, they have weaved such an intricate web of deception and gone to great lengths to attempt to destroy an individual's life. I am laughing at how silly the entire game is and when you see all of the hidden clues, you realise that the wickedness does not stop. Unfortunately, for the spell casters, the fact that the Creator sent in me a loving child of God to be the example.

We are living in a difficult transition right now and it is only with patience and self-control that we are able to re-position ourselves. As I sit here on the verandah enjoying the beauty of the island, the lavish scene, spectacular views, any attempt to thwart my happiness has been rejected. I didn't hold back from communicating to OJ that his full moon spell is null and void. Attempts to have me locked up in prison for his drug-related crimes are null and void. During my dream the same night, he tried to attack me and ran through the house in a rage.

God, the Creator of Heaven and Earth is the answer to the struggles, the minute that you hand things over they are resolved. The plan was for me to be killed or to have to murder and or traffic drugs, at least have drugs planted on me and then incriminated. Again, the Satanists underestimate my ability to see into the source of the plans and hand them back to the sender.

What is the mentality behind family sacrifice for fame and fortune? What would make the siblings so cold and unfeeling, pure jealousy. The bible from creation shows the relationship between Kane and Abel, we see Joseph sold as a slave by his family. In the same way, my family members attempted to sell me into slavery to reap my good fortune. God sees everything and saves me from any further persecution by taking me out of the worldly dynamics and negativity. The ascension came through right on time to lift me to a higher portal and take me out of the vacuum.

I started to attract new friends, who also vibrate on the higher plane, and build genuine relationships, finally starting to live the life that I deserved filled with happiness and adventure. We worry, feeling that we are too late or too early, the universe will always give back what we put in, no one has the power to change someone's destiny. The spell is a question for the transfer to go ahead, the individual's attention or acknowledgement is required. Without clear and direct verbal communication the laws will not stand. You have the free will to accept or decline, your silence is acceptance.

I trust in God to take care of all the minor situations for me. During this targeting, I have faced daily challenges, one after another, yet still, I rise.

Everyday challenges come at all from all different directions. No matter how well thought out the day is, we face adversity. The character that you build is dependent on how you face those issues. Do you shy away and lay in bed hoping that it will all go away or do you look it in the eye, head on and challenge?

Right now, we are going through one of the most problematic times in history with the BREXIT. 80% of the population have turned a blind eye and are hoping that it all works out. The only way it will work out is if we get involved and work it out. It is time for us to get off the fence and off the sideline and get in the middle. We are warriors, we can do this in a number of ways.

We can fight and kill each other, then who are we left with, the most physically strong or wicked. Alternatively, we can come together lovingly and help each other and learn how our thoughts and consciousness can impact lives. We can look to countries, groups, and communities and help them with practical methods to change their programming and the way they are living. The system is designed to control us and by now you will have worked that out. What we can do is change the system by changing the way that we approach situations. The programming, mind control, OZ programming, Disney programming. This is our one opportunity to turn it around.

If like me you are woke and realise that there is a power within us that is off the scale, then it is time to come together and use it. We plan different ways to change the frequency or vibration of the atmosphere with our thoughts. Whatever we believe is the outcome, and if we are conscious, we will understand where the dark energy is coming from and transmute it into positive. Nothing and no-one can stop positive actions if the reasons behind our judgments are made with integrity.

We often come into contact with people and cannot understand how or why we have this person in our life. Perhaps they reflect or mirror a part of us that is needing change or attention. By helping this individual soul and setting them free will also set you free, an opportunity to heal the fragment of your soul that has been distorted.

There is way too much noise in our society now due to technology and everyone is an influencer, but what are we influencing on Instagram. Pretty pictures are not an influence. It is time to form an allegiance with those that have experienced the toughest battles, where the fight has become a gridlock and influence change through compassion and understanding.

The Star Wars is over, there is no winner in this spiritual battle, just a lot of unhappiness and bloodshed, it is time for the wealth to be shared out amongst the poor, who have been robbed and used to set up schools and help convicts, drug addicts and the homeless back into the system. It is time to teach independence and sovereignty, it is time to ensure that those who are struggling due to lack of education or living in estates on a low income are considered and not harassed.

We are slowly killing ourselves through this NWO and the small percentage with the wealth are realising that the shift of power is real. The Creator is here and urging the population to take back the control of our precious earth. What are you afraid of? Nothing can hurt you; we have other beings that are working closely with humanity to put things right. They are picking the most humble, selfless people to lead.

Let the revolution begin, it Is time to say No to illegal house break-ins, no to bullying, no to black magic rituals, no to fear. It is time to say Yes to peace, love and higher consciousness. We refuse to be held down, beaten, persecuted and torn. The Brexit game is causing nothing but lack of confidence in trade, the thought of lack produces more lack, therefore we are caught in a vicious negative cycle.

Until we realise that money is not real and has no real value, only the value that we place on it, we will continue to travel down this road to a dead end. And I mean dead. During the targeting spree, the beings showed me clearly that remaining calm and sitting in a higher vibration is the only way to overcome the victimisation. If you choose to fight tooth and nail on their terms you are drawn further into the illusion. Focus your mind clear on what it is you desire and head for your dreams, do not allow negativity or hate to block or control you.

CENTURIES OLD MILAN

How did I manifest this? The opportunity to be with the wild and glamorous at a Milan fashion show after party and steal the show. Oh, how they enjoyed my see-through black gown, the look on their faces as the nipples popped out was hilarious. It was one way to get noticed and promote my business. I guarantee that everyone wanted to be the lucky person with the glamorous lady on his arm. As far as was concerned it was one in the eye for the handlers. I can imagine their jaws dropping, tongue salivating images. I casually hung around outside waiting for the arrival of the celebrities, only to find that those inside spent the majority of their day locked in their hotel rooms. No doubt keeping out of the eye of the press and relaxing. I noticed a tall, dark African looking model, she walked past me in the foyer and I recognised her as a perp. She sat to the left of the building on the wall, staring deeply into her mobile phone. I took this opportunity to approach her. "Excuse me, I love your look, how did you find the show? She immediately went into a very rehearsed script dealing with all the shows that she had attended and fittings, the fact that she had a driver, spent £2000 in Prada (her daily limit) and couldn't understand why the bank blocked her card. I casually asked 'would you mind me taking a picture for my blog.' She responded in a very polite manner.

Only on asking her name did I realise that she was a very down to earth celebrity who responded kindly to fans and admirers. A group of young people to the right of the Hotel congregated, these were fans of Nicky Minaj. They asked whether they could take photos. I was all for it, the more exposure the better to get my face known. The only way that I could see to prevent this racket from continuing was to carefully and systematically expose the culprits. Those who are well aware of the targeting of humanity and fueling the fire. I realised that the majority of perps were individuals who had been subjected to a horrific ordeal and found that they could do nothing more than join up to avoid further persecution.

People in my life who had behaved very strangely came to mind. Stephen Tagen and Freddie Clarke, those who refused to play the game died, others crossed over for the sake of peace.

This human experiment with people's lives was horrific and sadistic in every sense. My spirituality and down to earth approach to a life saved me from the misery it brought to others.

Getting to the crux of the system I realised that the earth we live in is nothing more than a human farm and we are the animals. We are expected to create a masterpiece. Whether it was art, story weighting, design or producing the next big thing. The world was in so much trouble on the edge of extinction. The only way to claw back was to turn to the creators and torment them to manifest. The fact that you kept a nice house and lived a quiet life was not enough.

All the months that I had spent listening to Hagmann and Hagmann, we had finally entered into the final no fear battle confrontation, the Star Wars battle had reached the final conflict. I had anticipated the time for the last few years, I had already changed my eating habits and the way in which I viewed money. Things had finally got to the point that we needed to win back the power that had been taken away over the last thousands of years.

I found myself passing titbits to my daughter, giving secondhand clothes to the poor, and never receiving second hood clothes. More importantly, help people. As many people as possible, we are the future of this planet, so we are responsible for the way it is treated. If we want it to change, we also need to fight for this change. Nothing is going to happen without our input. I realised that the time had come for action, it was time for me to assume my position and take back control of our land. I knew it would be difficult but the time away also gave me the new confidence that each individual plays a part.

A new strength was brewing inside me, I felt vigilant, almost vigilante and ready for action. The universe sent every form of evil to distract me. Getting back to the party, I casually introduced myself to Team 1. The perps work in teams.

It is so easy to spot them as they usually wear the colour red, or at least the main character is dressed in red, long red pants with her legs at least 6 ft tall. Masculine features and stature, it would be difficult to tell which sex she started her life as. Regardless they were all very friendly then came the young girl in the suit all alone.

The rather unusually tall lady asked me to come inside A grey, who knows? She wanted to introduce me to a designer, this was obviously the consciousness designer. Oh, what a surprise. Funnily enough, they all knew each other, now that was bizarre to many, not to me. I could see that they would lead me to team 2. We mingled and I introduced myself to various people.

Very nice I might add, a few invited me to parties and kept my number, however, it was the new MOL's role to introduce me to MR BIG. MR BIG 5ft nothing, why is it that the top mafia men are always short. He took numerous pictures with me; however, the plan was destined to fail as MR BIG was actually besotted with me. He looked at me and couldn't help but express his glee.

He arranged for us to go to dinner the very same evening, and he took great delight in showing me his castle and mentioning that he would hold a special party in my honor. Did I look like a dummy? Thanks for the invite, I'll pass this time on that wonderful offer. However, when you realise my abilities, I am sure that you will want to keep me around you for your own benefit. It was great at the party. By the way, let me tell you some of my favourite tricks. Umbrella rolled up, crossover bag, jumper over a shoulder, Coca Cola, cream pants, blue jackets, big logos on back for your attention only. Bare feet, bareback, I could go on. There are so many different ways that they try to mingle.

Unfortunately, once you understand the way this thing works you can spot the people involved. Orange bags, dry cleaning bags, black bags being their frequency, short trousers to show flood. Hand it all over to the father and spend no time worrying about it. It is so subtle and so clever. Hidden in plain sight.

The telephone casually ringing and conversations that would mean a great deal to you. Drinks with the words FUZE as fuck you ZE. It really depends on how you read the information and your mind, strength of character. H the letter 8 for infinity, 4 DNA and 14 the letter N. If you try to analyse all of it you end up nuts. Pink shoes, pink shirt reversing, give it all back to them in the name of Yahushua

As you observe them and see what the game is, it is amusing as the spirit of God locates them through your eyes and they know that you have noted who they are. They feel embarrassed and want to move.

The people involved are from so many different walks of life it is strange; they are all doing it for the same thing. Money. They need money so badly to go about their daily business and a lot of them are being blackmailed, they feel embarrassed but it is the only way out. Criminals are threatened with prison and other people who have a business and can't make money. The business isn't functioning the way that they want, alternatively they have made one sacrifice and didn't realise that they need to continue making the sacrifice. It is actually really sad that the world has come to this harsh reality. I feel very privileged to be in a position to express what is happening globally. It is no different in Italy than it is in Brussels.

The entire targeted individual concept dates back years, it is from generation to generation, the main focus tends to be an individual on a higher vibration. They encourage you to raise your vibration, they are already well aware of who the individuals are, natural born leaders with the ability to bring about a change in humanity. This program starts from the minute the child attends school. I spent a wonderful time in Milan, made friends with Daniela Bronco et al. The next stop was Brussels, what a dilemma. I spent more money in Brussels than during the entire trip.

The demons were certainly sitting close to my finances and draining every penny. From the cab ride that cost $150 Euro to the two cancelled hotel apartments totaling another $150 and finally the $50 dollar cab rides. The evil spirit was certainly in high spirits, this all came from the interaction and late meal with the Mafia boss, just as well I made excuses and left early. During the meal one member of the mob showed me his mobile phone and announced, "say happy birthday to Ricardo". The connection between Milan and the Millers.

Daniela stayed overnight as the cabman had charged an extortionate amount for the journey. Daniella pleaded poverty and I was in no state to leave her with him as he displayed signs of multi-personality disorder. He found it very challenging when I asked for our location. He twisted his head with rage and came to a sudden stop in the middle of the forest threatening to leave us. Still, it was all part of the experience. The flight that had been chosen for me flew from Milan to Brussels after a two-day stopover in Brussels on to Montego Bay, stopping to refuel in Cuba.

I quickly sensed that the next little set up was to make me out to be a drug trafficker. The only hotel within my price range and close by happened to be an old converted prison called the Lodge, my room number 306 was the only room left. The previous night the only room affordable was the Windsor room 33 which I swapped for a 23. They really went to great lengths to stitch me up. Even the food on the plane was loaded with NLP. Apple pie and a chocolate Twix, the extraordinary lengths that the shadow government would go to.

I can't imagine thinking of how much it must cost them to follow me around. What a star, really and truly I would have welcomed some privacy, but we get what we ask for. I felt it time to thank the Creator for the opportunity and focus my mind on building the refinery. I was charged up and mentally ready.

Nothing and no-one could stop me from this creation, it was so close I could taste it. I knew that NM and MD were part of the same syndicate gang but also realised that the economy would be challenged any day now and individuals were going to be happy to invest in an alternative type of wealth. The clock was ticking and I felt a sense of excitement that I had developed confidence and gusto to complete the challenge.

All roads had been blocked previously yet now it felt that all roads were open and my success depended on my ability. I had an audience keenly laying bets on my next move. It was a game of wits with your life and the winning trophy was your freedom.

He arranged for us to go to dinner the very same evening, and he took great delight in showing me his castle and mentioning that he would hold a special party in my honour. Did I look like a dummy? Thanks for the invite, I'll pass this time on that wonderful offer. However, when you realise my abilities, I am sure that you will want to keep me around you for your own benefit.

It was great at the party. By the way, let me tell you some of my favourite tricks. Umbrella rolled up, crossover bag, jumper over a shoulder, Coca Cola, cream pants, blue jackets, big logos on back for your attention only. Bare feet, bareback, I could go on. There are so many different ways that they try to mingle. Unfortunately, once you understand the way this thing works you can spot the people involved. Orange bags, dry cleaning bags, black bags being their frequency, short trousers to show flood. Hand it all over to the Father and spend no time worrying about it. It is so subtle and so clever. Hidden in plain sight.

The people involved are from so many different walks of life it is strange; they are all doing it for the same thing. Money. They need money so badly to go about their daily business and a lot of them are being blackmailed, they feel embarrassed but it is the only way out. Criminals are threatened with prison and other people who have a business and can't make money. The business isn't functioning the way that they want. Or they have made one sacrifice and didn't realise that they need to continue making the sacrifice. It is actually really sad that the world has come to this harsh reality. I feel very privileged to be in a position to express what is happening globally. It is no different in Italy than it is in Brussels.

I quickly sensed that the next little set up was to make me out to be a drug trafficker.

VOODOO

Voodoo is a religion. It is a criminal offence to use voodoo against an individual. This weekend they worked really hard to distort my senses, and are desperately trying to swap my soul with OJ. The Milan fashion show, meeting with the Mafia, the stint spent in the Hotel Prison plus the invitation to the Medical Marijuana and the Patricia Clark property in Jamaica.

As you can see, they have weaved such an intricate web of deception and gone to great lengths to attempt to destroy an individual's life. I am laughing at how silly the entire game is and when you see all of the hidden clues, you realise that the wickedness does not stop. Unfortunately, for the spell casters, the fact that the Creator sent in the company in the form of a God has affected their ability to weave the spell.

We are living in a difficult transition right now and it is only with patience and self-control that we re-position ourselves. I sat on the verandah enjoying the beauty of the island, the lavish scenery, spectacular views, it is clear that any attempt to thwart my happiness has been rejected. I didn't hold back from communicating to OJ that his full moon spell is null and void. Attempts to have me locked up in prison for his drug-related crimes are null and void. During my dream the same night, he tried to attack me and ran through the house in a rage.

God, the Creator of Heaven and Earth is the answer to the struggles, the minute that you hand things over they are resolved. The plan was for me to be killed or to have to kill and or traffic drugs, at least have drugs planted on me and then incriminated. Again, the Satanists underestimate my ability to see into the source of the plans and hand them back to the sender.

Why would a family ascribe a family member for fame and fortune? What would make the siblings so cold and unfeeling, it is pure jealousy. The bible from creation shows the relationship between Kane and Abel, we see Joseph sold as a slave by his family. In the same way, my family members attempted to sell me into slavery to reap my good fortune. God sees everything and saves me from any further persecution by taking me out of the worldly dynamics and negativity. The ascension came through right on time to lift me to a higher portal and take me out of the vacuum.

Targeting is predominantly witchcraft, the only way to deal with this is to raise the vibration of the planet. The intense harassment is for you to focus as much attention as possible and react to all situations. This will attract more of the same, so. you become caught in a cycle of abuse. The planet requires individuals to take this energy and transmute it into positive energy. The targets are isolated to prevent the strength in numbers. However, there is a great deal of power in the One. Do not feel that because you are alone you have no say or influence. The fact that your every thought is recorded clearly proves that you are of importance to the system. Sit back and allow God to take the lead, the Creator is working actively on your behalf even when it feels that you are alone. The more loving that you are and compassionate, the weaker the opposition becomes.

The system relies heavily on your energy, this energy is shared amongst those that are aligned with the beast. By being individual it causes a hole or vacuum where your spirit fits in, the connection that you have with the source is shared amongst the rest of humanity. You also benefit from this expulsion of energy. Take control of your own life, do not be afraid to be yourself. Do not play the role of victor, martyr or victim. We are shifting away from duality to oneness, where each person is important to the grand plan. The targets or those with the God genetic are important elements required to reshape the future.

Try not to be involved in the name calling or backbiting, sit in your own power. The money system is on its way to confusion, the best way forward is to disconnect from the ego and shift into just being. Technology belongs purely to the beast, do not be surprised if the phones are hacked, computers, bank accounts, this is the way of the world that we are living in. The so-called perps are other targets who are terrified and as such accepting the bribes. Again, this is just part of the way of the world. It is what it is, choose to live your life, follow your dreams and observe the changes.

Everyone experiences bad days, challenges, conflict; do not feel that you are the only person living in the drama. Try to understand from other people how they feel and their perception of what is happening. The Government has a script to follow and it is unfolding. Add to the positive where possible and disregard the negative. As system fails to exist then you treat it as irrelevant.

No matter how it feels as if you are in a tug of war, decide to follow your path. Seek out those individuals experiencing the same thing and empower them. Make them feel that there is hope and life is going to improve for all.

The situation is shifting as I change my perspective on the reality that we live in. The program is used to prevent humanity from upgrading their DNA and realising the power of intention and the word. The realisation that we can change our direction at any time. The AI is us and we are AI. The program is used to keep the old way of living which is now obsolete and moving towards extinction.

The news media is used to keep the illusion going, the internet, email, and instant messaging to shift your focus and prevent further ascension. Should this fail the telephone calls or text messages continue the process. The entire 'conspiracy theory' programme is polluted with false news to create situations. The only way through this is to stay focused and keep positive, we can share this energy with anyone.

The light and dark are battling for first place, we actually are watching a fusion of the two. Laugh at the situations that arise and overcome them.

I decided it was time to head back to the UK, funnily enough in the airport, my attention was drawn to a young boy crying and kicking his toys around. On a spiritual level, this was a reflection of Nicholas showing disappointment. I guess he was upset that I hadn't contacted him and the spell had no impact on me. As I walked through the tunnel to the plane the spilled milk on the floor symbolised that the milk had been spilled or spoiled.

The flight was full heading back to Brussels. A young lad from the north of the UK sat next to me, and a very interesting rasta travelling to perform in Brussels next to him. The young guy, I say young approx. 40 attempted to make polite conversation with me throughout the flight. What delighted me was the fact that he mimicked my every move. I drank water, he did the same, I read a few lines from a book, he pulled out a pad. He attempted to find out my destination to which I curtly responded "Brussels". He looked very similar to my nephew OJ. Oh my, the black magic was in full effect. I read the Lord's prayer and repeated scripture over him,

Fast forward to November, after days of sitting waiting for the winds to change, the opportunity arose for me to fly back to Jamaica. The guys from the recycling company were due to arrive in the Caribbean and wanted to meet me there. I was given five days' notice. So here I was, bills mounting up around me, bank accounts in the minus with five days to fly to the other side of the island. A difficult challenge for some, deep in my heart I knew that I would be there. Not a challenge for the brave and fearless. I called on a few of my dearest friends, raised the cash and off I flew.

Brussels airport, oh what a palaver! The airport failed to highlight the gate departure for the flight to Montego Bay until 15 mins before the flight was due to leave. The only issue was that gate 38 happened to be 9 mins from where I was standing. All would have been well if the assistant hadn't directed me out of the exit gate and back into the airport. The demons love to manipulate and show their power, the games the demons play.

I ran to the gate like a pig in heat, no stopping me now. I called the spirit world and requested backup.

My mind was set, I was heading to Jamaica to complete my project, nothing, no-one would prevent me from taking this opportunity. Good job that I ran the 3 miles in the UK without taking a break.

An orthodox Jew had pulled his baggage over my toes and pushed me out of the way. He wasn't my problem; I was set on course to change my reality.

I watched an older man hug his son, spiritually again this was the universe combined with the black magic peeking into alternate realities. I had to keep a clear head, a peep into another dimension representing sanitaria mingled with reality. By keeping calm, I could discern between the two.

I arrived at the gate only to find that one of the passengers had passed out and the health and safety team ran backward and forwards like the keystone cops flapping. This delayed the flight check-in. Thank you, Father.

On arriving at the airport, I called Porter to advise him of my arrival. In the background, a reggae song dedicated to me after the fall out with Nicholas was playing. I giggled to myself, "good just, bad justice, same just". Porter answered the phone and he sounded distressed. He sharply advised he was unable to collect me as he was unaware of my time of arrival and click, the phone receiver went dead.

As I handed the phone back to the taxi driver, I noticed my friend's husband standing next to me. We made eye contact; his first response was that his wife had been searching high and low for me. Without a bit of an eyelid, he whisked me off to his home. Dawn greeted me with hugs and kisses. God was surely working in my favour. The only person who can travel across the world and walk into friends, who express love, and prayer.

Monday morning at 9 am on the dot, I arrived at the villa much to the surprise of the Dutch guys. Lovely to see that the universe had arranged eye candy for me. Made the visit even more pleasurable. One of the very best days of the year, I fully enjoyed the freedom, renewed energy, and personal achievement. I knew that as long as I remained focused on the tasks, the universe would create the illusion. Absolute magic, the Creator within me and the divine combined the ingredients to produce the dreams that kept me focused during the more difficult months.

This is the end game for the planet and we are the generation that can bring it back to the beautiful place it was created to be. It doesn't require money, it requires thought.

THE ROOS GRIFTING IN THE NAME OF YESUS

"Praise the Lord, praise him". "I was a sinner, amazing grace" sang the Pastor. Ex gangster turned his life around to become an ordained clergy. Give thanks, what a role model. I met the pastor through a church sister, we sat in her shop putting the world to rights discussing the last days chronicle as per the King James Bible. How mixed up and contorted. King James as in the King in St James. "I am seeking souls for Christ Jesus" he acclaimed in his crisp Gucci jacket and matching shoes embellished with the sign of a sword on each foot. His casual every day going to church outfit. He was powerful, young people, desperate middle-aged women trusted him, believed in him, they put their faith in him. Even the believers who usually spend their tithe offering with the obeah man switched to the x gangster turned preacher. Why not, he praised God not the devil or so he genuinely believed.

We met a few times for chat, one particular Sunday afternoon we spent hours debating the word of God at his secret hideaway location, perched on a rocky ledge, approx. 20 ft above sea level overlooking the Caribbean Sea. Three white pigeons perched precariously over my head in a battered cage, beautiful views of the horizon, again a perfectly idyllic setting for romance. I giggled as I watched the man of God peak beneath my beach dress at the softness between my legs. "Hallelujah!" Man shall not live by bread alone.

Unmarried preacher, age 38 with children, child age 1, 3 baby mothers, 4 kids. Who am I to judge. Our jealous God Jehovah chose David from the sheep pen. Pastor was human after all conceived from a womb, only right he would want to remain close to flesh. Was he aware or asleep? After all he was being used to transfer energy, a player in the game of deception and witchcraft for money and power. He sincerely prayed for people and cast out demons, right? I watched his videos, seen the prophetess pronounce him. Do not touch my anointed ones do my prophets no harm.

We set off to St Mary for the ritual to begin. I knew it was a part of my targeting to lure me into a spell, intrigue got the better of me. We went under the guise of receiving deliverance. The church name 3 hills ran by the Chambers., On the way to the Chambers we passed a villa, 3 courts the name etched beautifully on the gate. Words used as spells to create the illusion of me being in court. Reminding me of the hotel converted from a prison in Brussels I spent a night in last September. I often wonder whether my mind is over active. Targeting requires spell casting and technology to keep the individual in a sleep state, The synchronicity forms the molecular structure of society.

The location of the church was very rustic, more of a converted barn than a traditional church, I expected to see a crib in the corner, and the pastor wife's singing could be heard as we approach from the road, albeit off key but all in good faith, "Lawd Gawd never leave no fo sake mi, mi Gawd" she howled in the name of sweet Jesus. The church greeted us warmly as we occupied our front row VIP plastic seats.

Testimony time. People took it in turns to bleat like the lamb of God, others sang songs of sorrow. "Press a lang saints, press a lang in Gawd's holy name, press a Lang..oh di arder di bakkil di sweeter di victory!" If it wasn't such a serious matter you would pee yourself laughing. I find this entire targeting programme surreal. I took the opportunity to share extracts of my story e.g., overcoming the obeah family sacrifice, battle with the 'gunman', car clutch sabotage, fighting for my soul. It seemed to resonate with the church as they stared at me in disbelief.

Actually, in retrospect it was probably my broad English accent. Here I was age 51 standing strong brimming with joy at the sheer adventure. I closed with "Jesus is a personal friend of mine and so is Pastor Shenanigans."

Next to testify, who else but Pastor Shenanigan, 5 ft 7 slim build, straight jawline, symmetric facial features, well presented, handsome. 9/10. Looks like someone I fell in love with; manipulation and occult magic running amok behind the scenes. He would be more suited to a boy band. He mesmerised the church with his testimony. Tears flowed from his eyes as he expressed the day the gun was put to his head and the trigger failed. What a performance, I was in awe. "He turned his mess into a message" his favourite quote. During his performance he stood in the sign of the cross, walked the floor between the isle, what a star! I envisioned him travelling the world testifying and gaining millions of followers on social media. Gun in one pocket bible in the other serving God instead of Satan, Still grifting a little but we all know God loves a sinner.

It came to offering time Pastor S handed me a 500 dollar note to place in the pink or blue bucket. Minutes later Pastor S walked through the doorway to the left and entered into conversation with one of the R Kerry minions in the white v neck T- shirt. White as in White House Government, T target. Pastor S motioned to me and asked me to hand over the 500 as he required change. He promptly handed the 500 to the perp. The Pastor handed me a different 500 dollar note as he returned to his seat. A few minutes later the perp returned a 500 dollar note to the Pastor. I thought he wanted change. Pastor placed this 500 in his wallet. Whilst the grifters carried out their little ritual I turned the bible to psalm 70, read the verse 3 times to break the spell casting. Followed by an additional psalm to hand the situation to the Creator.

Handling money is a transfer of your energy, this style of grifting is used to tap into your blessings. Pastor Shenanighan continued to wave notes around me as the service continued. 500 is a nanny as in nanny of the maroons, I am of maroon descent with the rebellious spirit of nanny.

"Does it matter where the money originates for tithe or seed? I mean even if the money is blood money or drug related will God increase it? I enquired. "How you mean? a money! it no matter it will manifest it is a seed" responded Pastor Shenanigan.

After approx. 15 mins after a young lady stepped from the pulpit walked directly into the congregation and handed a 500 dollar note to an overweight brown lady to my right, wearing a New Orleans t-shirt. New Orleans famous for its rituals and black magic. The usual suspects formed the perp group. Pregnant kitchen staff or chef behind me, feeding from my energy (chef 3856 1111 alpha numeric) duppy bowy at the back, bleach face behind him, enter posse in PINK. Laugh, it is so sad. I took out my iPad and recorded the entire church, it was so easy to spot the perps. As the Pastor called the congregation individually for prayers and deliverance, he warned all of the perps of impending death, lack of morals and ill fate, how bizarre! The perps are coerced into these roles or blackmailed, damaged souls, not all of them are wicked, each situation is different all carrying demonic attachments. They sold their souls; the Jinn use their bodies to manifest in our reality.

5.00pm my hour for deliverance. Pastor Shenanigans attempted to force me to stand behind the couple from Trelawny. I could feel their demons from my seat. I declined the order, " you must be obedient!" Pastor S declared. Rich coming from the Roo. 15 days of the month, sewing a 1000 seed 5.00

pm. The ritual had been so carefully orchestrated; I wonder who was the brains behind it from the 33-steering committee. I stood waiting patiently anticipating a thorough reading. The pastor had already mentioned names for others that related to me. Beverley, Melanie, Joseph family and friends working their science. Disappointingly he didn't have a great deal to say other than I would be hearing good news.

As I stood waiting for the reading known as a prayer (no different than a psychic reading) the witch with the New Orleans shirt rushed to stand behind me. Ugh! I could smell the stench of her spirits. I asked the Holy Spirit to travel with the 500 note and touch all the people who would come into contact with it.

Pastor Shenanigan is actually a lovely person, he was very kind to me throughout the day. It felt more like a date than a church outing. He walks quickly through the town as he is sensitive to energetic fields and vibrations still battling demons from his past. A highly spiritual being feeling stuck in a reality that he would prefer to leave. Next date is a day meditating in the mountains talking to God. Can't help wondering whether he will leave me there, throw me off a cliff or make love to me. Feels like I'm caught between the devil and the deep blue sea.

As I left the church, I noticed a huge sign with the name "Ray", name of the chief occultist involved in the manipulation. His signature sign confirming the deception as his handy work. Well done Ray - great job. Well done Kerry R Sandals marvelous work. Thank you for the money you sent today, hope all is well, the devil is a liar. Hallelujah.

Is Pastor Shenanigan a target, handler, perp or an individual trying to survive in our cruel world?

DOLLY

Why would he do it, I thought we were friends. Despite our difference religious beliefs, we had a mutual connection of respect and friendship. The local rum bar wasn't the type of place that I expected to frequent. But hey, Christ went into the most unusual places. There was no real reason to shine light in the church. So here I was chilling with the local rum heads. I still laugh at the fact I attempted to have normal conversations with them. The key reason I stopped going in was the voodoo doll. I loved the loud music; the waft of the passive ganja reminded me of my father and growing up. It took me straight back to the 70's only thing missing was the screaming and shouting. "You warra warra, no mek mi bum a rass cuss". That was the usual comment from my father during this time. I took control of the kitchen frying chicken and mixing the dumpling dough in the little shack serving shots of white rum and grab a. "Sell mi one Matterhorn". My regular perp, bless her she came in every hour or so. Slim, bleach black lips with long weave red hair. Red hair set the current trend. The usual suspects flocked around me as I took centre stage. As I danced to the reggae pumping from the radio and prepared the food.

Ilah and his brothers were devout Muslim. I think? Well at least they had the Muslim texts and appeared to speak with knowledge and wisdom. I reside in a small community, integration forming one of the most important aspects to me. Evenings were long, sunset at six thirty quickly becoming dark. We chilled a couple of evenings at fisherman's beach or as I would call it fisherman's bitch. I enjoyed the companionship of the opposite sex, having spent years alone it felt refreshing. On this particular evening I recall a few of my perps wandering around me one with a huge 'X' on his t-shirt, one shuffling sideways with an ex-military type gait. It was amusing to me as I continued to dance and goof around. The waves crashed against the shore an idyllic romantic setting for the right couple, it wasn't a romantic evening we were purely in the friend zone as far as I was concerned.

I heard a muffling sound which I believed came from one of the stray dogs. I crossed the beach in the dark towards the sound of the shrieks and sobs to find a stout looking man sitting on the side of a boat crying actually sobbing. My alpha male friend stepped back and allowed the matriarchal female to move forward towards the figure. I stood directly in front of him staring into his eyes. His clothing appeared neat yet his expression worn out, frustrated and agitated. I bent slightly to gain eye contact. enquired "How are you feeling." Daft question really it was pretty obvious he was borderline broken. As far as I was concerned it was a conversation opener. Bearing in mind it was pitch black, I didn't feel energetically that he was a threat more a fractured soul.

"I am talking to the Father" he replied. "I am asking for help". He went on to explain that life was extremely difficult for him. He lived in the ghetto on the opposite side of the road. Shack houses, 'poor' community, drugs and gun crime litter the streets in equal proportion to plastic bottle and black bags. Fragile violent family groups, basic education, male members easily drawn into corruption as a source of income. "I am faced with challenges weighing to heavy on me. I can't cope " he sobbed. He appeared to be around fourth, short in stature, dumpling face. He confessed that he made mistakes or made bad choices in his life. I found the entire experience disturbing. Strong black male completely shattered by life experiences howling in the dark. I felt spiritually that he had been involved with black magic, common in this particular community for power and protection. Hence, I didn't put my hands on him still I spoke to the Holy Spirit Divine intervention, the power is the Father, please console him. After some words of endearment and comfort I left the distraught guy holding a 'medi' and shifted back to my cosy spot.

What a coincidence, right time - who knows. Ilha remarked that based on our conversations prior to the incident we manifested the situation. Despite my Christian spiritual beliefs and his Muslim faith, we had stuff in common. Ilah wasn't the type to share his precious religious text books not that the teachings of Muhammad was my preferred bedtime reading. To be polite I accepted the copy only to return it the following day. The vibration from the book resulted in a sleepless night, chaos and confusion the following day.

...So why the voodoo doll. It was a Wednesday evening, middle of the week trying to organise a conscience movement decided to pop into the bar to discuss with a few of my radicals. Only to see a voodoo doll pinned to a nail on the wall. The low-down dirty bastard. "Oh, I see you made a voodoo doll of me!" Oh no, this is just a doll made of weed and rizla. Funny it is wearing my hair style. Honestly, it's not you, it's Tainer. He laughed trying to hide the embarrassment. Tainer peeped over the brim of his rum cup and kissed his teeth. It's obviously me, very funny. Ilha quickly removed the black cat cup from the corner of the room and entered the kitchen hoping that I hadn't noticed. I picked up the CD on the side by the door with "Follow di" written on it and the red stripe bottle in the corner. Simple everyday objects used to transfer energy. I smiled as he entered the bar from the kitchen. We both knew in that split second the friendship crashed and burned.

Ganja, weed, marijuana the portal or vibration used to pin me to the occult. My nephew had been a drug dealer for years. The ritual sacrifice required a transfer of lights or stars. The FA use light energy to feed the dark, global football or soccer appears simple but is complex in spiritual structure. The soul transfer success requires my vibration to remain in the gangster zone, hence the attraction to the twin flame gangster. Those within the cult enjoy an increase in power and finance for a period of time in return for their soul. To keep the level of wealth the initiates seek pure souls. We vibrate within two dimensions on one plane, light and dark within this illusionary planet earth.

ON RETURN TO THE UK

As I landed the Thailand airplane pulled in next to me. Nothing could prepare me for what came next. The powers that be had their hands and beady eyes on my bag.

THAILAND AIRLINE CRASH LEICESTER CITY

TO BE CONTINUED**

ABOUT THE AUTHOR

An extraordinary combination of born leader, entrepreneur, natural healer, mystic, author, activist and energy guru.... fully conscious black PEARL. Ms. Clarke born in the UK, DNA Jamaica WI from a young age felt a connection with other realms. Black Pearl transformation was founded after years of spiritual practice, working with angels, guardians and ET contact. Pearls are spiritual transformation. The metaphor is that the innocent, pure hearted, yet coarse grain of sand is transformed and slowly developed into an object of tremendous value and beauty. Pearls help us get in touch with the simple, honest things of life.

Targeted from birth, SRA victim, known in the UK as "Psychic Dee Clare", in Jamaica as "Tiffany" and the Ukraine "Ді Клер" placed her in the spotlight and the centre of mystic, magic manipulation and altered reality. Her experiences include face offs with the Italian mafia, Jamaican mafia and UK special branches. Throughout the most difficult times Diane held on to her beliefs in Christ Consciousness and

through her faith maintained her emotional stability. Diane shares her insight into aspects of black magic rituals that will amaze you, satanic ritual abuse and how it is used to influence society. How our leaders, politicians and those in positions of power are motivated and controlled by inter dimensional beings. Her knowledge and experience are likely to open your eyes to an entirely new world.

As we approach a shift in energy, change in consciousness, the planet is in need of high vibrational empaths for us to arrive collectively at a common goal of world peace and love.

Printed in Great Britain
by Amazon